Canada Close Up

Alberta

Katie Bailey

Scholastic Canada Ltd.
Toronto New York London Auckland Sydney
Mexico City New Delhi Hong Kong Buenos Aires

Visual Credits

Cover: Daryl Benson/Masterfile; p. I: Dorn1530/Shutterstock Inc.; p. III: A.G.E. Foto Stock/First Light; p. IV: (top left) Alan Gleichman/Shutterstock Inc., (top middle) Dumitrescu Ciprian-Florin/Shutterstock Inc., (top right) Trucic/Shutterstock Inc.; pp. 2-3: Leksele/Shutterstock Inc.; p. 4: Tyler Olson/ Shutterstock Inc.; p. 5: (bottom) W. Perry Conway/Corbis; p. 6: V. J. Matthew/Shutterstock Inc.; p. 7: CP Photo/Adrian Wyld; p. 8: (top) Thomas Kitchin & Victoria Hurst/First Light, (left) Mayskyphoto/ Shutterstock Inc., (bottom) Jackson Gee/Shutterstock Inc.; p. 9: Michael T. Sedam/Corbis; p. 10: Darwin Wiggett/AllCanadaPhotos.com; p. 11: CP Photo/Larry MacDougal; p. 12: Karl Naundorf/Shutterstock Inc.; p. 13: (left) John T. Fowler/Alamy, (right) Paul Lau/Shutterstock Inc.; p. 14: Dan Lamont/Corbis; p. 15: Dave G. Houser/Corbis; p. 16: (top) Wayne Lynch/AllCanadaPhotos.com, (bottom) Tim Thompson/Corbis; p. 17: Carson Ganci/Design Pics/Corbis; p. 18: IPK Photography/Shutterstock Inc.; p. 19: (top) Roderick Chen/AllCanadaPhotos.com, (middle) Sinclair Stammers/Science Photo Library, (bottom) Photoresearchers/First Light; p. 20: DK Limited/Corbis; p. 21: (top) AF 83, quilled shirt, Siksika, late 19th Century, buckskin, porpucine quills, hawk bell, hair, feather, tin, cones, glass beads, pigment, Collection of Glenbow Museum, Calgary, Canada, (bottom) 60.45.1, Gerald Tailfeathers, "the Kill", 1960, tempera on paper, Collection of Glenbow Museum, Calgary, Canada; p. 22: Paul A. Souders/ Corbis; p. 24: (top right) Glenbow Archives, (bottom left) North Wind/North Wind Picture Archives; p. 25: Department of Immigration, Canada (Publisher); p. 26: Glenbow Archives; p. 27: (top) Glenbow Archives, (bottom) Henri Julien/Glenbow Archives; p. 28: Canadian Pacific Archives Image no. NS.16354; p. 29: A.Bruce Stapleton/Glenbow Archives; p. 30: Canadian Pacific Railway Company/ Glenbow Archives; p. 31: Glenbow Archives; p. 32: Mcdermid Studio, Edmonton, Alberta/Glenbow Archives; p. 33: (top) Glenbow Archives, (bottom) Barrett & MacKay Photo/AllCanadaPhotos.com; p. 34: Tibor Bognar/Corbis; p. 35: Randy Lincks/Corbis; p. 36: Jack Dagley Photography/Shutterstock Inc.; p. 37: Claude Robidoux/AllCanadaPhotos.com; p. 38: Natalie Fobes/Corbis; p. 39: (top) Rolf Hicker, (bottom) John E Marriott/AllCanadaPhotos.com; p. 40: Courtesy of the Village of Glendon; p. 41: Raymond Gehman/Corbis; p. 42: Steve Degenhardt/Shutterstock Inc.; p. 43: (top) Subbotina Anna/Shutterstock Inc, (middle) Glenbow Archives; back cover: Videowokart/Shutterstock Inc.

Produced by Plan B Book Packagers
Editorial: Ellen Rodger
Design: Rosie Gowsell-Pattison
Special thanks to consultant and editor Terrance Cox, adjunct professor, Brock University;
Tanya Rutledge; Jim Chernishenko

Library and Archives Canada Cataloguing in Publication

Bailey, Katie
Alberta / Katie Bailey.
(Canada close up)
ISBN 978-0-545-98901-5

1. Alberta--Juvenile literature.
I. Title. II. Series: Canada close up (Toronto, Ont.)

FC3661.2.B345 2009   j971.23   C2009-900236-1

ISBN-10 0-545-98901-9

6 5 4 3 2 1   Printed in Canada   09 10 11 12 13 14

Contents

Alberta's provincial bird is the great horned owl.

The provincial flower is the wild rose.

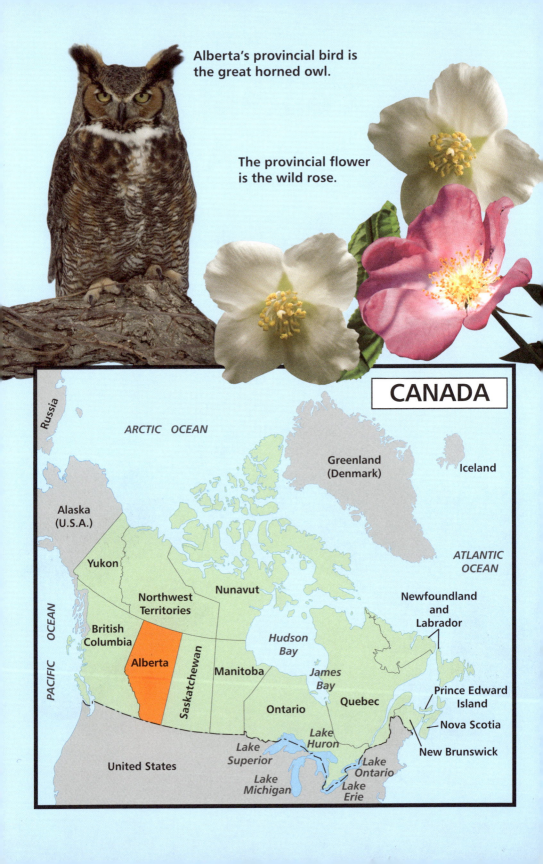

CANADA

ARCTIC OCEAN

Russia

Greenland (Denmark)

Iceland

Alaska (U.S.A.)

Yukon

Nunavut

Northwest Territories

ATLANTIC OCEAN

Newfoundland and Labrador

British Columbia

Alberta

Saskatchewan

Hudson Bay

Manitoba

James Bay

Quebec

PACIFIC OCEAN

Prince Edward Island

Ontario

Nova Scotia

Lake Huron

New Brunswick

United States

Lake Superior

Lake Ontario

Lake Michigan

Lake Erie

Welcome to Alberta!

Alberta is a province of towering mountains, open plains and great forests. It is home to a world-famous rodeo and some of Canada's biggest cattle ranches and farms. Beneath the ground are the **fossilized** remains of dinosaurs and the world's second-largest oil **reserves**. For the 3.45 million people who live here, it is a place of adventure, opportunity and riches.

Alberta is one of Canada's western provinces. It shares vast grasslands, covered in wheat fields that stretch as far as the eye can see, with its fellow prairie provinces – Saskatchewan and Manitoba. These relatively flat lands give rise to forest-covered foothills, followed by majestic mountains – the famed Rockies – on the British Columbia border. Throughout its history these rugged, untameable landscapes have helped define the province as Canada's true wild west.

So grab your hat, pardner, it's time to explore Alberta!

Chapter 1
Plains, Peaks and Permafrost

Alberta is a place where many different landscapes meet. Its prairies are part of a longer swath of grasslands that extends from southern Alberta, Saskatchewan and Manitoba to Texas in the southern United States. The Rocky Mountains, which Alberta shares with British Columbia, follow a similar path. They are part of a chain of mountains that form the western backbone of North America from Alaska to Mexico. Northern Alberta is covered in low-lying marshes and permafrost.

The prairies

Most of southern Alberta is prairie, made up of flat land or gently rolling hills. Ten thousand years ago, glaciers covered this area. As these giant rivers of ice receded, they flattened the ground. They also left behind **sediment** that had been trapped in ice. This made the prairie soil good for growing crops today.

The prairie is very dry. When moist air from the Pacific Ocean rises over the Rocky Mountains, its moisture is lost as rain or snow. The air that comes back down on the other side of the mountain is warm and dry. This creates an area called a rain shadow, which includes most of Alberta.

Chinook winds

When a warm wind blows down from the mountains in winter, it is called a chinook. A chinook can melt snow and raise winter temperatures by 20 degrees Celsius in one hour!

Just north of the prairie lies the most densely populated area of Alberta. Here, human settlement – farms and towns – competes for space with prairie grasslands and aspen forests. The climate here is cooler, and the weather is slightly damper than on the prairie.

ALBERTA

NORTHWEST TERRITORIES

Wood Buffalo National Park

Lake Athabasca

Peace River

River

Fort McMurray

Athabasca

Grande Prairie

River

Athabasca

St. Albert

★ Edmonton

Jasper

Jasper National Park

Mount Columbia

Red Deer

Banff National Park

Drumheller

Lake Louise

Red Deer R.

BRITISH COLUMBIA

Canmore

Banff

Calgary

N

Alberta Badlands

Head-Smashed-In Buffalo Jump

Medicine Hat

0   100 KM

Fort Macleod

Lethbridge

ROCKY MOUNTAINS

SASKATCHEWAN

The endangered burrowing owl makes its nest in abandoned fox, badger or ground squirrel holes on the prairie.

The badlands

In southeast Alberta the prairies suddenly drop off into a vast, dry land of canyons, caves and strange rock formations that some people say looks like a bizarre alien world. This is the Alberta badlands!

Over thousands of years, erosion helped shape the badlands. Water and wind gradually carved away at the surface, leaving layers of **sedimentary rock** exposed. Coulees, or deep ravines that cut through the landscape, were created long ago when glaciers unleashed great stores of meltwater that had been trapped in ice.

Hoodoos form when wind and water wear away the soft rock at the base and leave behind the hard rock that sits on top.

The boreal forest

Most of Alberta is covered in boreal forest. In the northern boreal forest the trees are conifers. These types of trees, like spruce and pine, have needles instead of leaves. Farther south, the boreal forest is mixed with aspen and poplar trees, both of which have leaves that change colour in fall. The forests are home to black bears, wolves, coyotes, elk, deer and moose, as well as many different types of owls. Although more trees and plants can grow here than on the prairie, the climate is still dry. Forest fires are common, but the plants are hardy and regrow quickly.

A helicopter drops flame retardant, used to control the spread of fire, on an Alberta forest.

The Rocky Mountains

Over millions of years, two gigantic pieces of Earth's crust pushed against each other and rose into craggy peaks. These are the Rocky Mountains, on Alberta's western border. The peaks are very cold and snow stays on them year-round. Some animals, like the sure-footed mountain goats and bighorn sheep that perch on the steep cliffs, have adapted to life here.

At the base of the Rocky Mountains lies a series of rolling hills called the foothills. Here, grizzly bears make their homes in the cool climate and mixed forests of lodgepole pine, spruce, poplar and aspen trees.

Glaciers and rivers

Most glaciers melted thousands of years ago, but some remain today. The Columbia Icefield lies between Mount Columbia and Mount Athabasca in Jasper National Park, in the Rockies. From here, eight massive rivers of ice, including the Athabasca Glacier, creep down the mountains. As they melt, some glacier water feeds rivers, like the Bow, North Saskatchewan and Athabasca rivers.

The Columbia Icefield

The north

In northern Alberta, summers are short and cool and winters are long and cold. Some of the ground is frozen year-round, in a state called permafrost. It is so cold here that snow stays on the ground for up to eight months of the year. When the snow melts in spring, some of the ground becomes wet and waterlogged, creating marshes and swamps. Wolves hunt here and moose and caribou browse for food. Birds of prey, such as bald eagles and peregrine falcons, snatch fish from the rivers and marshes.

Hot springs and hailstorms

- With an area of 661,190 square kilometres, Alberta is Canada's fourth-largest province.

- Alberta is one of only two **landlocked** provinces. The other is Saskatchewan.

- Banff National Park, in the Rockies, was Canada's first national park. It is famous for its hot springs – pools of water naturally heated by the Earth.

- At 3747 metres, Mount Columbia is the province's highest point.

- The meltwaters of the Columbia Icefield eventually flow into three oceans: the Pacific, Arctic and Atlantic.

- Alberta gets more hailstorms than anywhere else in Canada. Sometimes the hailstones are as big as golf balls!

A large hailstone

Chapter 2
A Land of Plenty

Alberta is the wealthiest province in Canada because of all its "black gold," or oil. It has the most oil reserves in Canada, and the second-most in the world. The oil industry employs about 300,000 people and brings in almost half of the province's money. Oil is a valuable **fossil fuel** – it is used to power automobiles and industries, and to make plastic, chemicals and paint.

Pumpjacks, or "nodding donkeys," dot the Alberta landscape. They are used to bring oil to the surface. This one is surrounded by a brilliant yellow **canola** field.

Natural gas

Alberta also produces about 80 per cent of Canada's natural gas. Natural gas is a colourless, odourless gas that is processed and used for heating homes. Alberta's natural gas is sold to the rest of Canada and the United States. It gets to where it is needed through pipelines.

For Albertans, the natural gas industry means lower heating bills, but it also means jobs and money for the government. The **royalties** that the natural gas and oil companies pay to the Alberta government are used to fund roads, schools, hospitals, the arts and much more.

Alberta's prairies are a popular location for wind turbines because of the dry, windy climate. Wind turbines are used to generate electricity.

The **Alberta Hub** links 500,000 kilometres of natural gas pipelines. That's a lot of pipe!

Oil sands are scooped out of the earth using digging machines that create huge open pits.

Oil sands

Some of Alberta's oil is expensive and difficult to get out of the ground. This is because it is trapped in oil sands – a mixture of clay, water, sand and bitumen. Bitumen is a thick, heavy form of oil. To extract the oil, powerful steam or chemicals are used to separate it from the sand. The three main oil excavation areas are located in central Alberta. They are the Athabasca, Peace River and Cold Lake oil sands.

In total, there are about six million cattle on Alberta's farms.

Farm fresh

Agriculture is Alberta's second-largest industry. Almost all of the prairie is used as farmland. On prairie farms, people raise cattle, chickens and pigs or plant crops such as wheat, oats, barley, canola and peas. Alberta is Canada's second-largest grain producer, but the crops need help to grow in the dry climate. Farmers must use **irrigation**. Albertan farmers started using irrigation in the late 1800s. Today Alberta is the most irrigated province in Canada.

Beef is Alberta's top agricultural **export**. Forty per cent of Canada's fifteen million cows, bulls, steers and calves are in Alberta. The beef industry includes raising the cattle on large ranches, but also butchering and packaging the meat, which is shipped to the rest of Canada and around the world.

Alberta laws state that logging companies must plant new trees within two years of harvesting an area.

Forestry

Over 60 per cent of Alberta is covered in thick forests. The forestry industry here has two main parts: harvesting the trees and making them into products. Alberta's forest products are transformed into **pulp** and paper, lumber for construction and finished products such as cabinetry and furniture.

The Banff Springs Hotel is one of Canada's most popular tourist destinations.

Tourism

Millions of people from all over the world visit Alberta every year. They come to see the spectacular Rocky Mountains, spend time in the beautiful national and provincial parks or experience Alberta's vibrant culture. Tourism brings in about $5 billion a year.

A snowboarder performs a spectacular jump at an Alberta mountain resort.

Chapter 3
Dinosaur Discoveries

Alberta was a much different place 75 million years ago than it is today. Most of southern Alberta was covered by a great sea called the Bearpaw Sea, and dinosaurs roamed the land. Today the province is one of the best dinosaur fossil discovery places on the planet!

The bones of more than 35 different species have been discovered in the Alberta badlands, including *Tyrannosaurus rex*, duck-billed *Hypacrosaurus* and *Triceratops*. Alberta even has several dinosaurs named after it, including *Albertosaurus sarcophagus* – a meat-eating dinosaur that looked like a small *Tyrannosaurus rex* – and *Triceratops albertensis*.

The soft rock of the badlands is constantly being worn away by wind and water to reveal new dinosaur bones.

Albertosaurus

Since the 1800s, over 300 dinosaur skeletons have been found in Dinosaur Provincial Park. It is one of the world's richest sources of fossils from the Cretaceous Period, 144 to 65 million years ago.

The fossilized remains of dinosaur bones are removed from the ground by paleontologists.

The bones are carefully reconstructed and displayed at a museum like the Royal Tyrrell Museum near Drumheller.

From the work of paleontologists, we can guess what dinosaurs such as the duck-billed *Edmontosaurus* might have looked like. But no one knows for sure about the skin!

Alberta's fossil riches

Alberta's most important fossil is not *T. rex,* or even *Albertosaurus.* It is the stromatoporoid, an ancient dome-shaped, sponge-like creature that lived in the Paleozoic Era, 590 to 248 million years ago. It is this creature that is mainly responsible for Alberta's oil wealth today.

Stromatoporoids lived in the water and grew by continually discharging a hard, calcium-based substance from their bodies. This substance formed huge reefs in the Bearpaw Sea that attracted other ancient sea creatures. When the seas disappeared and the landscape changed, the reefs were buried deep under rock. As millions more years passed, the weight and heat of the Earth turned the remains of the reef creatures into oil.

A stromatoporoid fossil

Chapter 4
Frontier Alberta

Aboriginal peoples have lived in Alberta for thousands of years. In the south, the Blackfoot Confederacy was the largest group. It was made up of three nations: the Siksika, Kainai and Piikani. They lived in small groups called bands, following and hunting herds of bison.

A Blackfoot shirt decorated with dyed porcupine quills

The buffalo hunt was important to the survival of plains Aboriginal peoples.

Head-Smashed-In Buffalo Jump, near Fort Macleod

At Head-Smashed-In Buffalo Jump in southwest Alberta, herds of bison were chased off a cliff. At the bottom, hunters carved up the dead beasts, putting every part to use for food, tools, weapons, clothing, shelter or trade items.

Like the Blackfoot, the Cree who lived on the plains led a **nomadic** lifestyle, hunting bison and living in tipis on bison migration routes. Aboriginal peoples living farther north, including Cree, Beaver, Slavey and Chipewyan peoples of the forests, hunted and fished along the region's many lakes and rivers.

Early contact

European trade goods reached Alberta's Aboriginal peoples before Europeans did. Explorers traded knives, cloth and kettles for food and furs. These goods were then traded between different Aboriginal groups. Even animals were traded this way. Spanish explorers introduced horses to Central America and the southern United States and traded them with the Aboriginal peoples there. In time, the horses reached the prairies and became an important part of the lives of the Cree and Blackfoot.

Fur trading

The first European to record his travels to modern-day Alberta was Anthony Henday in 1754. He worked for the Hudson's Bay Company, which had been established in 1670 by King Charles II of England. The king's cousin, Prince Rupert, was the company's first governor. The company's **charter** gave it the right to trade for furs over an area that covered present-day Manitoba, Saskatchewan, Alberta and parts of Ontario and Quebec. This area was called Rupert's Land.

Fort builders

Two fur trading companies competed in the west in the 1700s: the Hudson's Bay Company and the North West Company. Each built forts for trading furs with the Aboriginal peoples. The first fur trade fort in Alberta was Fort Chipewyan on Lake Athabasca, established by the North West Company. From here, explorer Alexander Mackenzie set out to find a route to the Pacific Ocean, a task he successfully completed in 1793. Also working for the HBC, and later the NWC, explorer and mapmaker David Thompson created the first maps of Alberta and the Rockies.

The currency of the fur trade was a Made Beaver, or a fraction of it. One Made Beaver token was was equal to one prime beaver skin.

The *coureurs des bois* travelled from Montreal to trade with the Aboriginal peoples for furs. Many of them later became part of the North West Company.

The Northwest Territories

Despite the thriving fur trade, the West had few settlers outside the fur trading posts. The Hudson's Bay Company didn't want settlers living in its trading area, so it told everyone that the West was unsuitable for settlement. That changed in 1870 when the government of Canada purchased Rupert's Land from the company. The government named its new land, excluding Manitoba, the Northwest Territories.

To encourage settlement, the Dominion Lands Act of 1872 was passed in Ottawa, offering 160-acre (65-hectare) parcels of land for just $10 each.

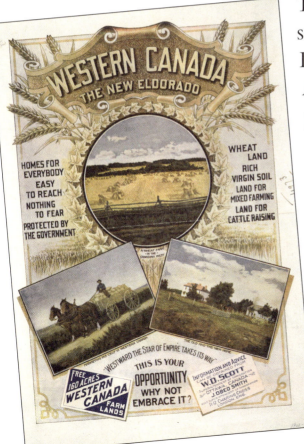

An advertisement encourages settlers to move to Alberta.

On a mission

Catholic priests often travelled with the fur traders. Their job was to convert Aboriginal people to Christianity and pave the way for new settlements. Father Lacombe, a priest from Quebec, came west to the prairies in 1849. He lived and preached among the Cree and Blackfoot of Alberta for most of the following 50 years. A man who loved travel and adventure, he created schools, industries, transportation routes and an agricultural colony, and improved relations between the Aboriginal peoples and new settlers.

A mission, or Christian base, near an Aboriginal settlement

Fort Whoop-Up was a trading post run by whisky traders from America. It was infamous for being wild and lawless.

Law and order

A bloody battle between American whisky traders and the Assiniboine in the Cypress Hills in 1873 proved the need for law and order. A new police force was created and sent west in 1874. It was called the North West Mounted Police. It later became the Royal Canadian Mounted Police (RCMP).

A railway west

It took many weeks for settlers to travel overland to Alberta from the east. A railway would make it faster and easier to move people and goods across the country. The Canadian government hired the Canadian Pacific Railway Company to build one. Tempers flared at the decision to run the railway through southern Alberta, rather than farther north, near Fort Edmonton. The settlers of the more-populous north felt that the government had ignored them. The railway was completed in 1885. More settlers began to move to the frontier to settle the land, building farms and ranches.

This Canadian Pacific Railway car was used to entice settlers from the east to move west. It was packed with western-grown wheat and vegetables.

The signing of a treaty between the Blackfoot and the Canadian government.

Signing treaties

Life had changed for the Aboriginal peoples of Alberta. The bison had been hunted nearly out of existence and the people lost their most important food source. Without food and with the loss of their territory to the new settlers, their traditional way of life was in danger. The Canadian government made agreements, called treaties, with Aboriginal leaders. In return for ownership rights to the land, Aboriginal people were to receive assistance in building new lives on **reserves**.

Although some Aboriginal leaders did not want to sign the agreements, they did so to prevent their people from starving. The first agreement, called Treaty Six, was signed in 1876. It applied to the Cree people who lived in central Alberta. Treaty Seven was signed in 1877 between the Blackfoot and the government. Treaty Eight was made in 1899 with the peoples of the north.

A province is born

As settlements grew, the leaders of Canada realized that the Northwest Territories was too big to govern. Alberta and Saskatchewan became separate provinces in 1905. Alberta was named after Princess Louise Caroline Alberta, daughter of England's Queen Victoria. Edmonton was chosen as its capital.

In the early 1900s, farmers from Europe were encouraged by the federal government to immigrate to the West.

The government worked hard to encourage immigration. Americans, Ontarians and Europeans, especially Germans and Ukrainians, were invited to move to Alberta. People with farming or trade skills were especially valued. Chinese immigrants, who had first come to British Columbia to build the railway there, moved to Alberta once it was completed to find jobs.

A family of Ukrainian settlers

Ten thousand workers and unemployed gathered for a mass demonstration in Edmonton in 1932.

Tough times

In the 1930s the **Great Depression** crippled Alberta's economy and forced farmers into poverty. The price of wheat, Alberta's main export, dropped from $1.27 a bushel in 1928 to just 30 cents four years later. To make matters worse, parts of Alberta were in a **drought**. The land dried up and turned to dust. The wind blew the dust into fierce storms that blackened the skies and coated everything in sight with dirt. Some farmers lost so much money they abandoned their farms and headed east to find work.

Oil is discovered at Leduc.

Black gold

The fortunes of Alberta changed when oil was discovered in Leduc, Alberta, in 1947. Companies came to Alberta to search for more oil, creating many new jobs. The government earned money from the oil industry by taxing the companies. The city of Calgary became the business hub of the oil industry, while Edmonton became the centre of oil-industry product manufacturing. Today people from all over the world come to Alberta to work in its oil industry.

Calgary's Pengrowth Saddledome is shaped like a giant horse saddle.

Chapter 5
Spirit of the West

Half of all Albertans live in Alberta's two biggest cities: Edmonton and Calgary. The rest live in smaller cities, like Lethbridge, Red Deer and Medicine Hat, or in or near the many smaller towns and villages around the province. Some places, such as Banff, Jasper and Canmore, are prized for their location in the Rockies, while others attract people with their industries, like Fort McMurray in the Athabasca oil sands.

Alberta's first city

Edmonton is Alberta's second-largest city and its capital. It began as an HBC fort in 1795. Today, you can visit a reconstruction of the fort and experience the life of a fur trader at Fort Edmonton Park, located just outside the city. A modern city attraction is the famous West Edmonton Mall, one of the world's largest shopping centres. It is so big it even has its own indoor roller coaster!

Calgary

Its nickname may be Cowtown, but Calgary is Alberta's largest and most populous city. In 1988 it hosted the Olympic Winter Games. You can still visit venues built for the Games, such as the Saddledome, now used by the Calgary Flames hockey team. At Canada Olympic Park, lugers, bobsledders, skiers and snowboarders take advantage of the ski hill, half-pipe and bobsled-track facilities.

The Calgary Stampede

Ten-gallon hats and cowboy boots can be seen everywhere during the Calgary Stampede. This ten-day festival of rodeo events, parades, concerts and festivities is the world's largest outdoor rodeo and brings over a million people to Calgary each summer.

At rodeos, people show their skills in ranching tasks and western-style horseback riding. Rodeo events include cattle roping, wild bronco riding and barrel racing. But one of the Stampede's most exciting and dangerous events is the chuckwagon race. A chuckwagon is a covered wagon pulled by a team of four horses. In frontier days, chuckwagons carried food, the cookstove and other equipment on cattle drives. The first chuckwagon race took place at the 1923 Calgary Stampede. Today, to win the $500,000 prize, chuckwagons are pulled along the track by thoroughbred horses while thousands of screaming fans cheer from the stands.

Mountain sports

The Rocky Mountains are a playground for people who love the outdoors. Skiers and snowboarders come from all over the world to visit Alberta's many ski resorts. The biggest mountain resorts are located near Banff and in Jasper National Park, the largest national park in the Rockies. In summer, people hike on the mountain trails or go mountain climbing.

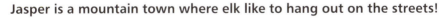
Jasper is a mountain town where elk like to hang out on the streets!

Ukrainian dancers in costume perform beside the world's largest *pysanka* in Vegreville, Alberta.

Small-town living

Life in Alberta's small towns is much different than it is in Calgary and Edmonton. Often a community was settled by a single ethnic group. Life was centred on traditions from the home country. Today Alberta's small towns are more diverse and people often work in local industries such as ranching, forestry or oil. Although many of the small businesses that once made up their bustling downtowns are now gone, local festivals and agricultural fairs still celebrate Alberta's rich ethnic past.

One such festival is the Pysanka Festival in the town of Vegreville. A *pysanka* (peh–SAHN-kah) is a Ukrainian Easter egg. During the festival, people can sample food and music from the Ukraine. They can also make their own colourful *pysanka*.

Medicine Hat is one of Canada's sunniest cities and is home to the world's tallest tipi.

Grain elevators line the highway into the farming community of Milk River.

Tasty Alberta

Steak is Alberta's most famous food. People all over the world enjoy the tender beef that comes from Alberta's cattle ranches. Bison meat is also popular in Alberta, as well as elk. Farmers in Taber in the south claim to grow some of the best sweet corn in Canada. The long hours of sunshine and cool nights of the region bring out the natural sugar in the corn, making it extra sweet. The weather here is also just right for potatoes. Almost 100 different kinds of potatoes are grown in Alberta today, most of which are made into french fries or chips.

Food is big in Alberta. Or at least food statues are! Check out this 2.7-tonne steel perogy in the village of Glendon! Other large foods include a 12.8-metre-tall kielbasa in the town of Mundare and the world's biggest mushrooms, standing 6 metres tall, in the village of Vilna.

Alberta's Aboriginal heritage

The fabric of Alberta's identity is tightly woven with its Aboriginal peoples. The province has 47 First Nations and the largest population of **Métis** in Canada at 67,000. Some of Alberta's Métis live in settlements established as long ago as the 1930s.

One of the best ways to experience Aboriginal culture is to attend a local powwow, a celebration of singing, dance, art and performance. The Siksika of the Blackfoot Confederacy hold a three-day fair and powwow every summer. It is one of the biggest in the province.

Chapter 6
Points of Pride

▶ Canada's most famous women's rights activists all lived in Alberta. In the early 1900s they fought and won a legal battle to have women recognized as people under the law. The Famous Five are Henrietta Muir Edwards, Nellie McClung, Louise McKinney, Emily Murphy and Irene Parlby.

▶ Wood Buffalo National Park was created in 1922 to protect free-ranging bison, or buffalo.

▶ Jerry Potts was a Métis guide in southern Alberta in the 1800s. He helped the North West Mounted Police choose the site for Fort Macleod and remained with the police as a scout, translator and guide for 22 years.

▶ Alberta has lots of bees and the most beekeepers of any province in Canada. Together they produce about 30 million pounds of honey per year.

▶ In the late 1800s, John Ware became Alberta's first black cowboy. Born into slavery in the United States, Ware moved to Canada, where he became a well-respected cattle rancher.

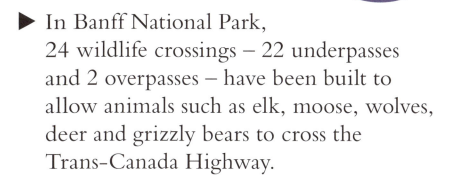

▶ In Banff National Park, 24 wildlife crossings – 22 underpasses and 2 overpasses – have been built to allow animals such as elk, moose, wolves, deer and grizzly bears to cross the Trans-Canada Highway.

▶ Computer scientist James Gosling, from Calgary, is credited with developing the computer programming language Java. Java can be used to create games, power websites or control electronic devices.

Glossary

Alberta Hub: A natural gas storage facility at Peers, Alberta, midway between Edmonton and Jasper

canola: A grain that produces a low-acid oil

charter: A grant of rights, signed by a king or queen

drought: A long period without rainfall

export: Something sent to another country, usually for sale

fossil fuel: A fuel formed over long periods of time from the remains of living things

fossilized: Turned into stone while embedded in rock

Great Depression: An international economic crisis (1929-1939) that left many people out of work and very poor

irrigation: Supplying land or crops with water, often by channels or pipes

landlocked: Entirely enclosed by land

Métis: People of mixed Aboriginal and European ancestry

nomadic: Moving to different locations throughout the year

pulp: A soft mass of ground wood fibres used to make paper

reserves: (p. 1, 12) Extra amounts for future use; (p. 29) Designated land set aside for First Nations peoples to live on

royalties: Payments made for the ongoing use of something

sediment: Matter carried along and deposited on the surface of the land

sedimentary rock: Rock formed from sediment, often in horizontal layers